HAPPY TIMES WITH HAPPY SEEDS

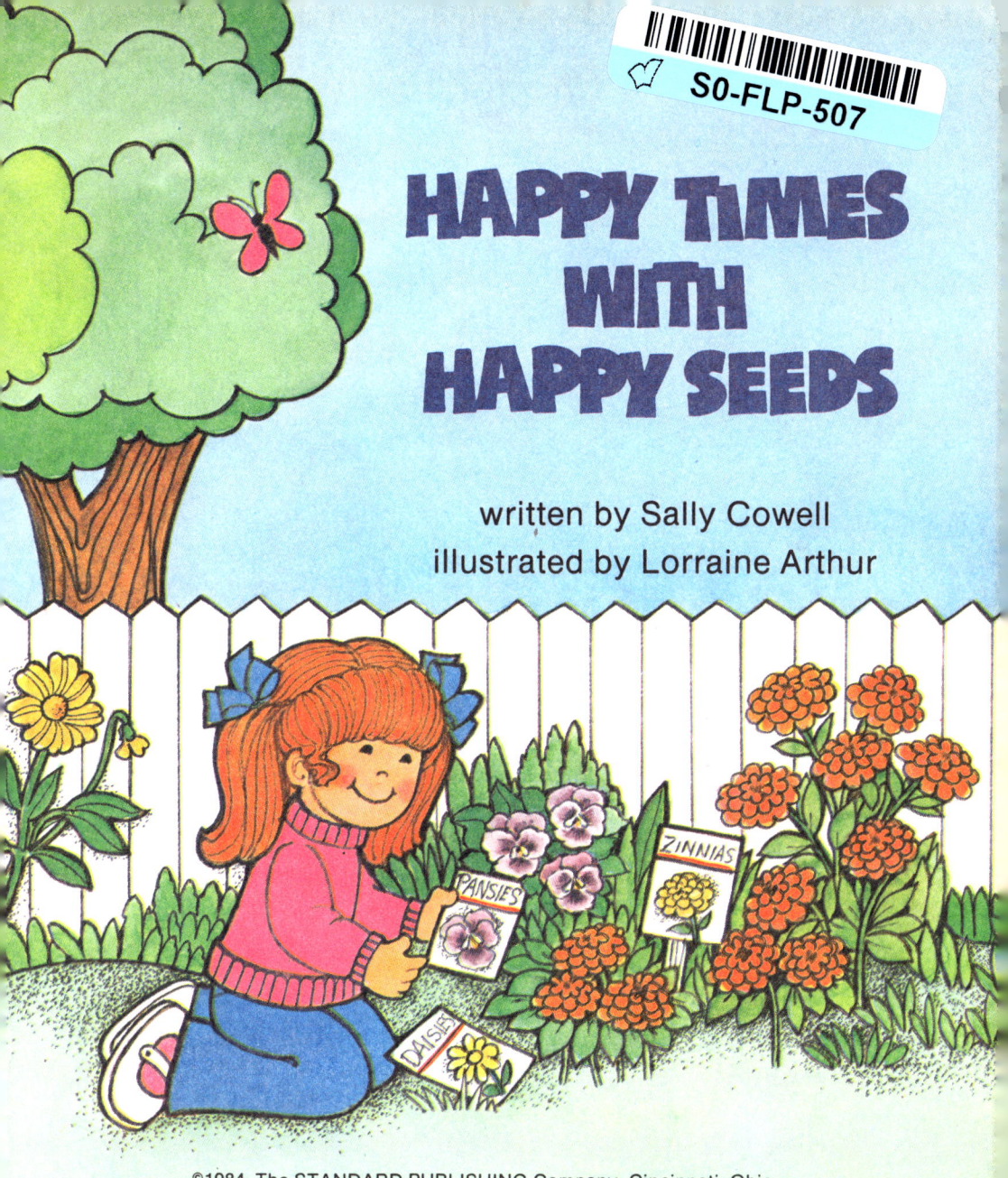

written by Sally Cowell
illustrated by Lorraine Arthur

©1984. The STANDARD PUBLISHING Company, Cincinnati, Ohio
Division of STANDEX INTERNATIONAL Corporation. Printed in U.S.A.

The distinctive trade dress of this book is proprietary to Western Publishing Company, Inc., used with permission.

Happy seeds do not grow into tomatoes.

They do not grow into apples,

SPINACH

or flowers.

I can't buy them in a little packet at the store,

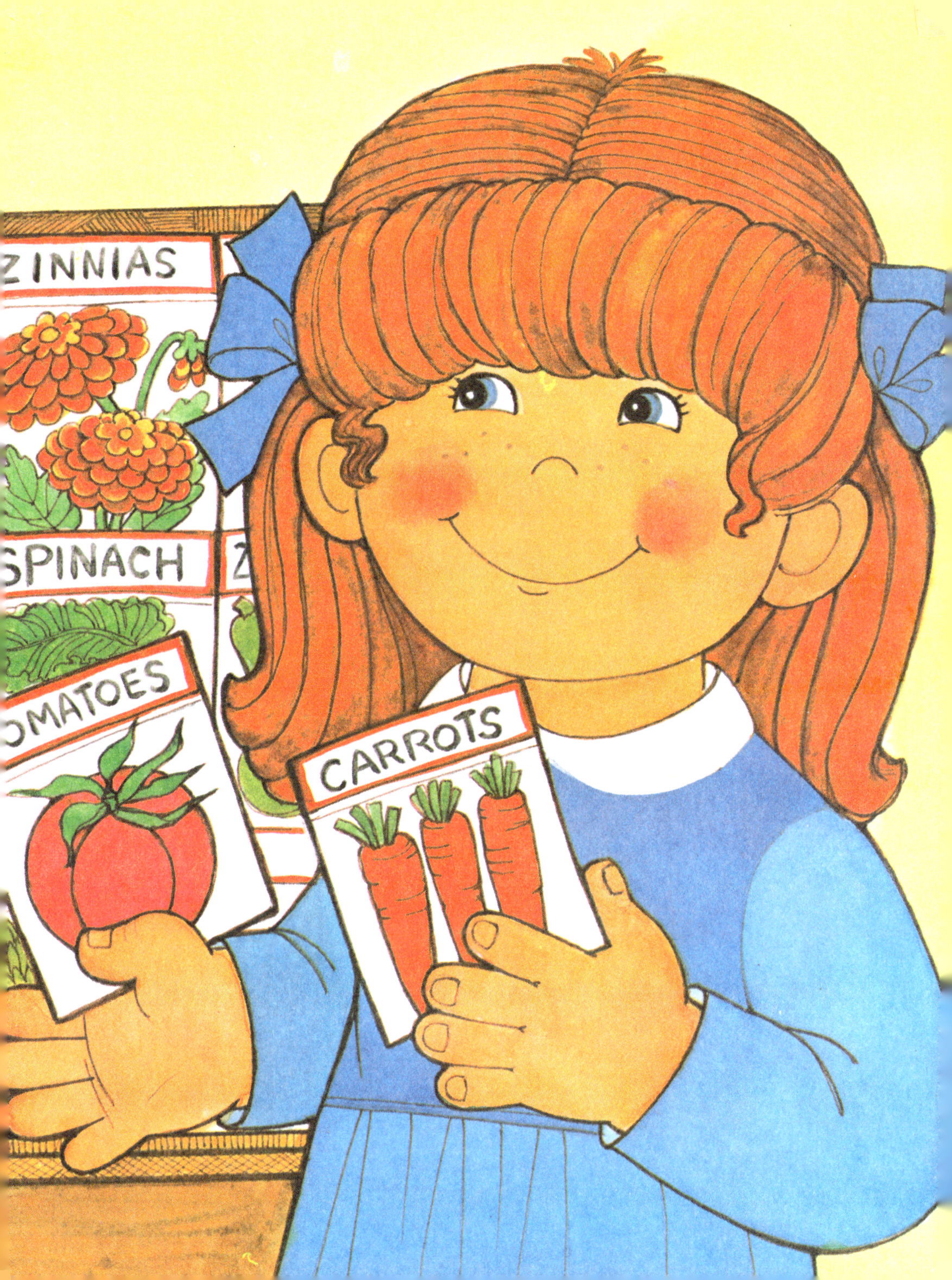
ZINNIAS
SPINACH
OMATOES
CARROTS

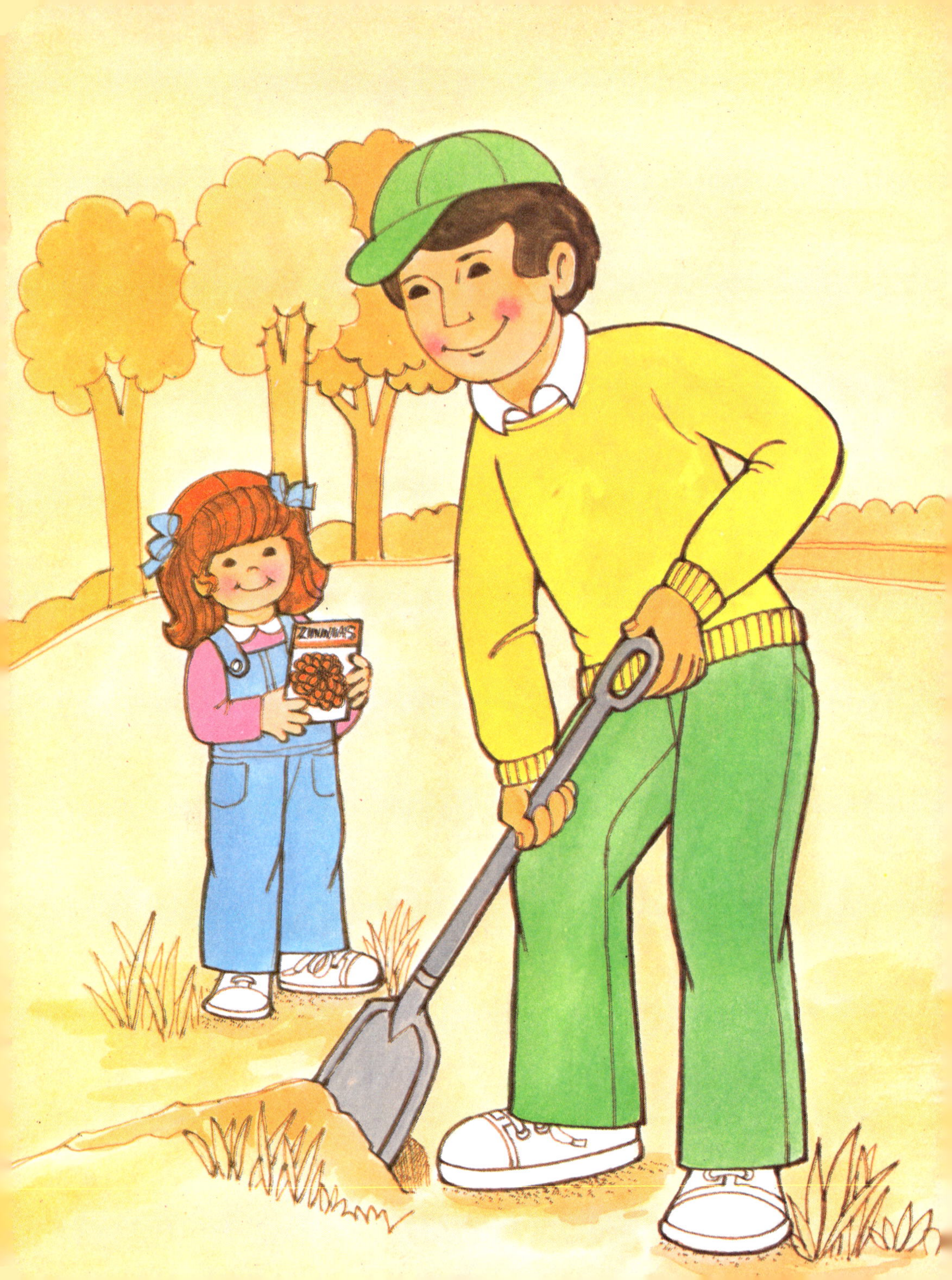
ZINNIAS

or dig a hole and bury them in the garden. But . . .

I can plant them just about everywhere,

all day long,

even when it's snowing.

I planted some happy seeds when I smiled at

my new friend,

the mail lady,

my teacher,

my little sister,

EVERYONE!

When I said, "I'm sorry," (and meant it) to my brother, I planted a happy seed.

And I planted one when I hugged Daddy and whispered in his ear, "I love you!"

POTATOES
APPLES
CORN
10¢ EAR
BANANAS
20¢ LB.
WHEAT CEREAL
CRACKERS
COOKIES
JUICE
PEAS
PICKLES

And still another when I didn't beg again and again for a gum ball after Mother said, "Not this time."

I like to grow zinnias,

pansies,

squash,

and peas.

But it's even more fun to have happy times

and good friends

by planting lots

of happy seeds!